Everyone Communicates
Learn how to talk to ME!

The guidebook to communicating and socializing with nonverbal and limited communicators

Barbara Huntress Tresness

Copyright © 2015 by Barbara Huntress Tresness

All Rights Reserved. No part of this book may be produced or transmitted in any form or by any means, electronic or mechanical, including photocopying, recording or by an information storage and retrieval system—except by a reviewer who may quote brief passages in a review to be printed in a magazine or newspaper—without permission in writing from the publisher.
Chat Collective, Inc.
100 Clinton Avenue
Fayetteville, NY, 13066
www.chatcollective.com

First Edition: November 2015
Published in North America by Chat Collective, Inc.
ISBN 978-0-692-49138-6
1.   Parenting & Relationships - Special Needs
2.   Parenting & Relationships - Parenting
3.   Children's Books - Special Needs
4.   Children's Books - Education & Reference

Comments and requests for additional book copies of Everyone Communicates: Learn how to talk to ME! , book club rates and for author speaking appearances, direct inquires to Barbara Huntress Tresness at www.chatcollective.com
Other books by Barbara Huntress Tresness: Beyond a Charmed Life, A mother's unconditional love

Forward

This how-to guide for the verbal community will help readers understand and appreciate what it means to communicate using a range of communication styles. It is full of insights and practical ideas. The Yes/No Hand Bands that Barb Tresness has developed are a great way to communicate simply and effectively in any setting. These Hand Bands are also a really great way to show awareness and support for inclusion. Imagine an entire classroom showing their commitment in this way!

Nienke P. Dosa MD, MPH
Center for Development Behavior and Genetics,
Department of Pediatrics, SUNY Upstate Medical University

Note to Reader

Thank you for taking the first step to communicate.

Thousands of people in this world who have challenges communicating because of disabilities or accidents, strokes, traumatic brain injuries, ALS, etc. Simply labeling them "nonverbal" suggests there isn't or shouldn't be any hope for communicating with them, which is why we advocate using the terms "Limited Communicator" (LC) or "Nonverbal Communicator" (NVC).

The premise of this guidebook is to showcase that we all have the ability to communicate, in some way. You might be a mom looking to communicate with your child with autism. Maybe you are a family member looking to share a special moment with a parent/grandparent who had a stroke. You could be a therapist/educator desperately trying to communicate with the student in front of you. This book can provide some guidance. I penned this book for those of us longing to communicate with our children, our parents, and all those with limited communication skills.

We hope you'll join us in changing how these children and adults are described because we believe this is the first step toward changing the way they are treated. And ultimately, that is what drives CHAT Collective: to Connect Humans through Awareness and Technique.

With gratitude,

Barb

Barbara Huntress Tresness
Author and disability advocate
www.chatcollective.com

Dedication

I dedicate this book to Graham Chamberlain Tresness.

Trapped in a body that does not work the way you might like and unable to communicate in a typical way: it was as if you were in a cage.

I had to find a way to unlock what was inside of you so the world could know what was inside. I knew you were there and I never gave up trying to reach you in whatever way I could.

Just like a bird that learns to fly and gains freedom I have watched you learn to use an eye gaze technology computer to free yourself from the cage. Today you are a confident communicator with a great sense of humor. You find new ways to let your personality show, give your opinion, advocate for yourself, even yell at your mom when she forgets to ask your opinion first or let you make the decision on your own. You told me the words I never thought I would hear from you. That beautiful synthetic voice said "I love you".

I am so proud of your strength. You survived years of people who could not see or hear you, keeping you in the cage, and fought hard for your freedom.

You found your voice and it has been incredible to watch you fly!

There are lots of ways to say hello

Hi! How are you?

How's it going?

Hey!

Hola!

What's up?

Como estas?

But what if you could not use your voice to say hello?

How else could you do it?

You could smile or wave your hand.

You could fist bump or nod your head.

You could write hello on paper, on your tablet or computer or communication device.

You could hit a button called a switch that will activate a prerecorded message on a device that says hello for you.

You could use your eyes to choose to say hello on a computer by looking at the word hello . . .

That is called eye gaze technology.

What is communication? Lots of things!

Crying is communication.

Instead of
"Stop crying" or "what's wrong?"

Reframe it.

How about
"I hear you"
or
"What are you trying to tell me?"

Behavioral outbursts can also be about communication. What if we asked a student or child what they are trying to tell us when there is a behavior that is difficult before trying to stop the behavior? What if we tried to figure out why the behavior happened? If we looked at the behavior as telling us something, what would it be?

What is Hand Talk?

There are many ways to talk with your hands. Some people talk with their hands by gesturing. Some people who are hearing impaired might use American Sign Language or lip reading to communicate.

Barb learned how to communicate with her son Graham in so many new ways. So she started CHAT Collective and penned this guidebook, with the desire to share communication experiences and help others. **This guidebook is to help others learn more about communication with nonverbal and limited communicators.**

This is Graham

Graham is a Nonverbal Communicator or NVC. He uses AAC or Augmentative and Alternative Communication to talk. He uses a device to talk as an alternative to speech. Graham uses eye gaze technology to talk.

Nonverbal Communicator (NVC):

We call someone a nonverbal communicator when they cannot use their voice to talk.

People who are nonverbal communicators still have thoughts, ideas and feelings to express just like you do. They need help to communicate. They use alternative ways to talk. Devices like switches, tablets and computers help or assist them.

Limited Communicator(LC):

Some people have limited communication skills.

What does that mean?

We call someone a limited communicator when they can use their voice to talk but only in a limited way.

Their voice might work but they can only say a few words or their words might be hard to understand. They need help to communicate too. They need devices to help augment or assist their limited speech.

Augment means more help in addition to the limited amount they can do or say.

AAC=Augmentative and Alternative Communication

AAC users usually use devices like switches, tablets or computers to help them communicate their thoughts, ideas and feelings to classmates, family and friends.

Sometimes AAC can be called Assistive Technology. Sometimes AAC can be called Adapted Technology. Sometimes AAC can be called Augmentative and AlternativeTechnology. It can be very confusing but it all means the same thing.

Who can remember all these words?

Help is on the way.....

A special kind of teacher called a speech and language pathologist (SLP) can help a nonverbal or limited communicator learn to communicate.

An SLP (Speech and Language Pathologist) is a therapist who can help you find the device that will help you communicate.

The ducks show different beaks (big ones, loud ones, soft ones, small ones) symbolizing that each of us communicates in a unique way.

Which device will become your voice?

You can ask for an evaluation, or an appointment to try different devices.

It takes a special person to understand that everyone communicates.

It's important to work with someone who has experience with AAC devices as you make this important decision.

AAC users are limited by their devices. The device has to be programmed to have words to choose from. Can you imagine how it would feel if your favorite color is purple but you could not tell anyone?

What if someone asked you "What's your favorite color"? But the only choices on your device were red, yellow, green or blue. You would not be able to answer that question, and might not respond.

People might not understand that you don't want to answer because your answer is not on your device. They might misunderstand you and think you do not know how to answer the question. That would be really hard!

You might feel mad or sad that no one understands you. You might feel frustrated that you could not say purple because it was not programmed on your device.

It's important to continually program an AAC device to prevent frustration and enable the person to grow.

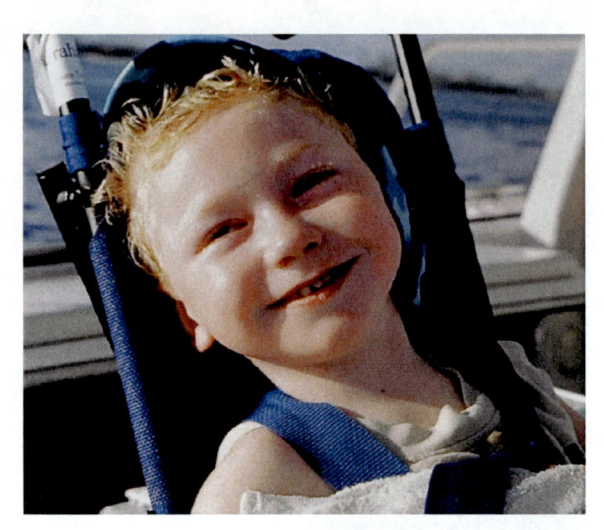

Barb with her son Graham.

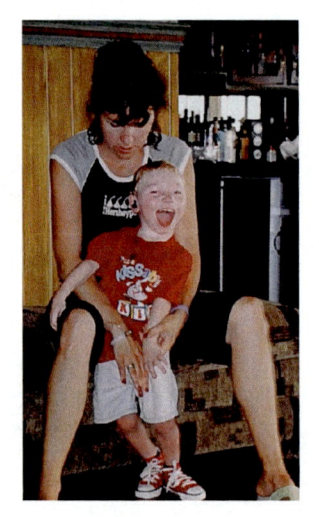

21

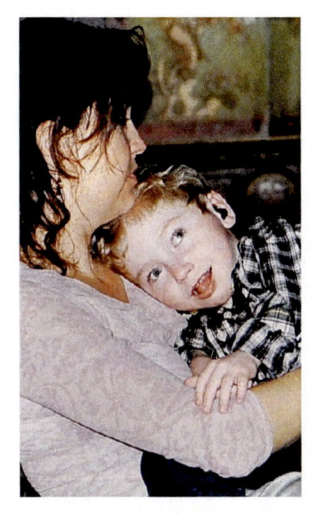

This is Kate.

Kate is a Limited Communicator. She is a college graduate, and is able to communicate in English, German and American Sign Language.

Kate uses an AAC (Augmentative and Alternative Communication) device to help her communicate. Kate uses her device to augment her speech.

Barb met Kate in 2012.

"We started as strangers, became colleagues and co-workers and great friends!" said Barb.

"Let me tell you a story about my friend Kate" said Barb.

One day Kate was at the dentist. She was busy typing on her tablet the message she wanted to say. The staff person yelled at Kate and told her to put the tablet away so the dentist could examine her. Kate was mad. The staff person did not know Kate used the tablet to augment her speech (AAC).

Kate needed a way to let people know she uses her tablet to talk. Barb gave Kate some communicator cards and she keeps them with her to pass out with her personal business card.

The **Communicator Cards** can be passed out to friends, family, teachers, dentists, doctors and others throughout the verbal community.

There is also a custom **Communication Profile Card** that can be personalized with greater details about communicating with an individual who is a NVC/LC. That profile card can be downloaded for free by visiting our website at **www.chatcollective.com**

"I created these cards to help Graham and Kate and other NVC/LC's identify themselves as communicators to the verbal community" said Barb.

Hi, I'm a Nonverbal Communicator
We All Communicate:
Learn How to Talk to Me.

chat COLLECTIVE WWW.CHATCOLLECTIVE.COM

* Please talk directly to me.
* I may need extra time answer you so please be patient.
* My computer/tablet is my voice. Please do not handle/use it.

To create your own detailed, personalized communication card, visit our website: **WWW.CHATCOLLECTIVE.COM**

Hi, I'm a Limited Communicator
We All Communicate:
Learn How to Talk to Me.

chat COLLECTIVE WWW.CHATCOLLECTIVE.COM

* Please talk directly to me.
* I may need extra time answer you so please be patient.
* My computer/tablet is my voice. Please do not handle/use it.

To create your own detailed, personalized communication card, visit our website: **WWW.CHATCOLLECTIVE.COM**

CHAT Collective is busy building tools and techniques . . .

Help is on the way.

It's as simple as YES or NO

Use the Hand Bands to Hand Talk!

The CHAT Collective **Hand Bands** are designed to be easily used by the verbal community to communicate with Nonverbal (NVC) and Limited (LC) Communicators.

The CHAT Collective Hand Bands can be used to ask **YES**/**NO** questions by holding the Hand Bands or wearing them. By asking questions that could be answered by looking at or touching the Hand Bands, many people will learn a new method of Hand Talk.

Hand Bands

Learning to ask questions that require simple **YES** or **NO** answers is a valuable skill for anyone who needs or wishes to converse with a nonverbal or limited communicator.

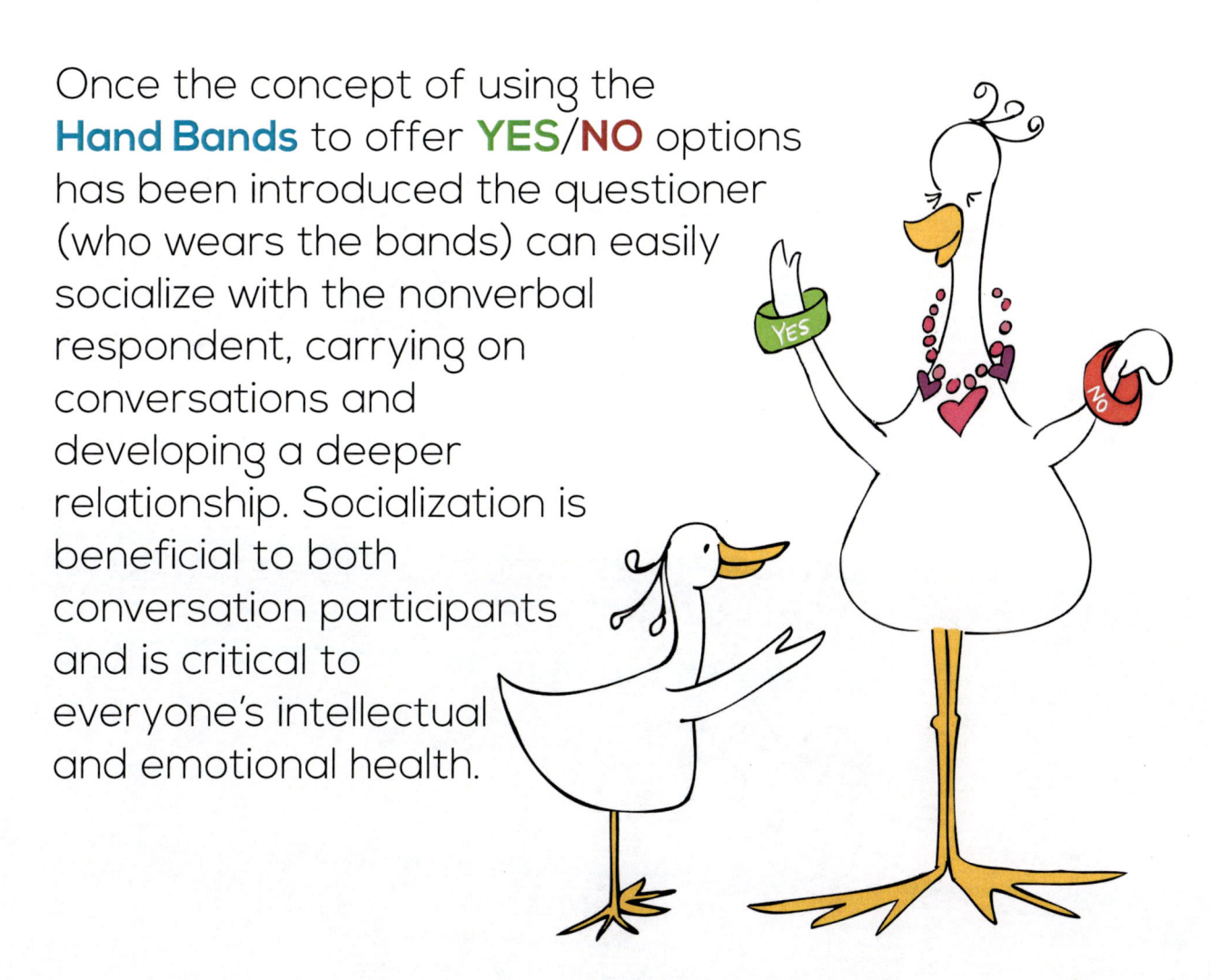

Once the concept of using the **Hand Bands** to offer **YES**/**NO** options has been introduced the questioner (who wears the bands) can easily socialize with the nonverbal respondent, carrying on conversations and developing a deeper relationship. Socialization is beneficial to both conversation participants and is critical to everyone's intellectual and emotional health.

How to get started

"I have these yes/no wristbands that I would like to try to use with you today.

This green one means 'Yes.'"
(Shake the wrist with the green band and make sure the person looks at it. Ask a clearly true statement, e.g., "Am I a person? **YES**!").

"This red one means 'No.'"
(Similarly, shake the other wrist with the red band and make sure the person can see this. Ask a clearly false statement, e.g., "Am I a frog? **NO**!")

Next, confirm that the person can identify the correct color and meaning of the bands by putting your hands behind your back for a moment, then presenting both options to the NVC/LC.

"Can you find the green 'Yes' wristband for me, please?"
Wait for visual, physical or verbal confirmation. Repeat with the other choice. When the person successfully locates the yes and no bands you are ready to use our product to communicate.

Now, simply ask **YES**/**NO** questions and have fun!

Let me show you how.

Do you like sports?
YES or **NO**

The person could answer by nodding their head
YES or **NO**
or saying the words
YES or **NO**.

But what if the person is nonverbal like Graham? You might need to offer choices that help someone know how to answer:

"Graham, look at me if your answer is yes.
Look away if your answer is no."

Or if the person can move their hands you could write the words **YES** and **NO** on two pieces of paper, hold one in each hand and ask them to touch **YES** or **NO**.

Or someone could look at **YES** or **NO** to give their answer. Or you could use Hand Bands and ask them **YES** and **NO** questions.

This can work for a friend or family member who is unable to talk or limited in the words they can say.

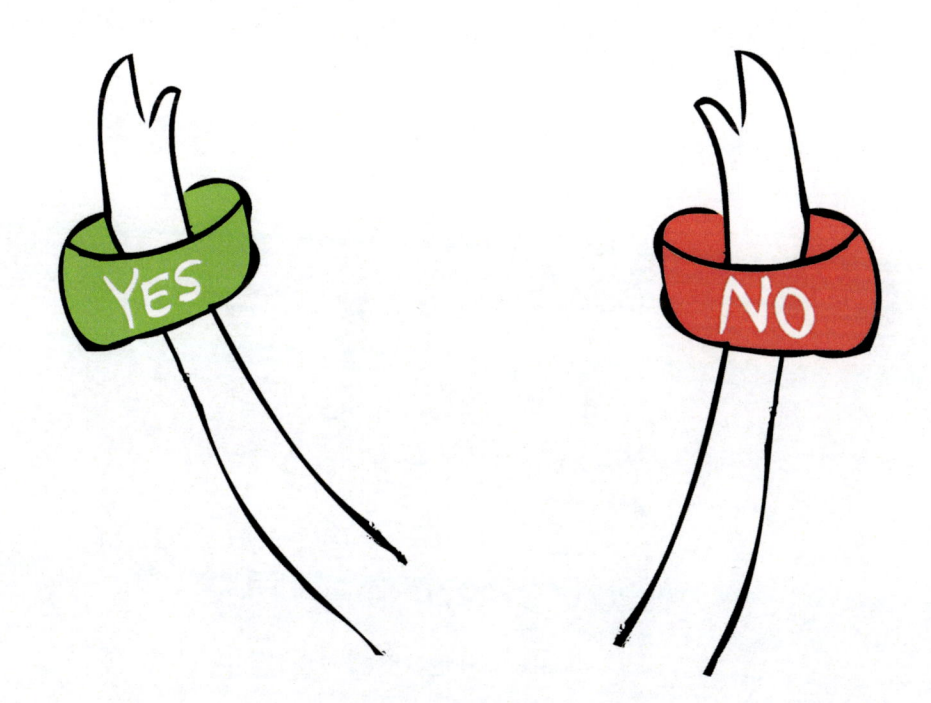

The following are sample YES/NO questions for common situations and conversation topics:

Meals and dining:
Instead of "What is your favorite food?" ask "Is pasta your favorite food?"

Other examples:
Do you like this restaurant? Food?
Are you hungry? Thirsty?
Do you want chicken?
Are you all done?

Other people:
Instead of "Who are your friends here?" ask "Is Bill one of your friends?"

Other examples:
Is Julie nice to you?
Do you want to see your cousin?
Do you know that person?
Do you remember Charlie?

Pain or injury:
Instead of "How do you feel?"
ask "Do you feel OK?"

Other examples:
Are you in pain?
Does it hurt when I push here?
Did this hurt yesterday? Two days ago?
Do you understand why I'm doing this?

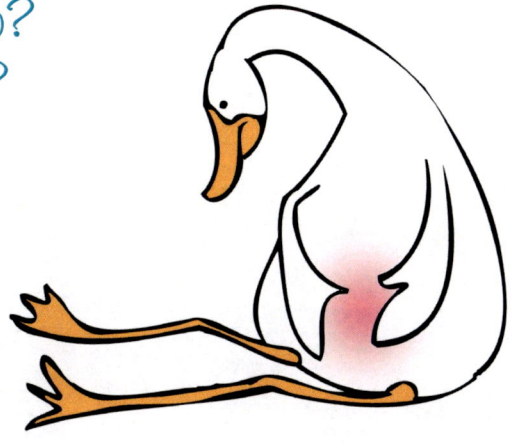

Shopping:
Instead of "What do you want?"
ask "Do you want me to buy some bananas?"

Other examples:
Do you need more tissues?
Do you like clothes shopping?
Do you like the red one better than the blue one?
Do you have enough money to purchase that?

School:
Instead of "Where do you go to school?" ask "Are you in school?"

Other examples:
Do you like school?
Do you like reading better than math?
Is your teacher nice?
Do you understand this question?

Hobbies/interests:
Instead of "What do you like to do?" ask "Do you like to watch game shows?"

Other examples:
Is "Frozen" your favorite movie?
Do you want John to do this with you?
Do you want me to read a book to you?
Are you better at this than your brother?

Sporting events:
Instead of "Who is your favorite team?"
ask "Do you like the blue team better than the red team?"

Other examples:
Is your team winning?
Did you like to play soccer?
Do you know someone on the team?
Do you understand the rules?

General conversation:
Instead of "How are you?"
ask "Are you having a good day?"

Other examples:
Are you happy?
Do you like the weather today?
Do you like this place?
Do you want me to help you with that?

If you have **Hand Bands** with you it is possible to communicate where ever you are!

In the car, in the pool, in the rain, in the snow, during gym or physical therapy . . .

Even if you have a device, they sometimes break or the batteries drain . . . **Hand Bands** always work. **Hand Bands** can help you communicate in more places than you can with a device. They can be quicker, easier and more fun to use!

Everyone likes to socialize!

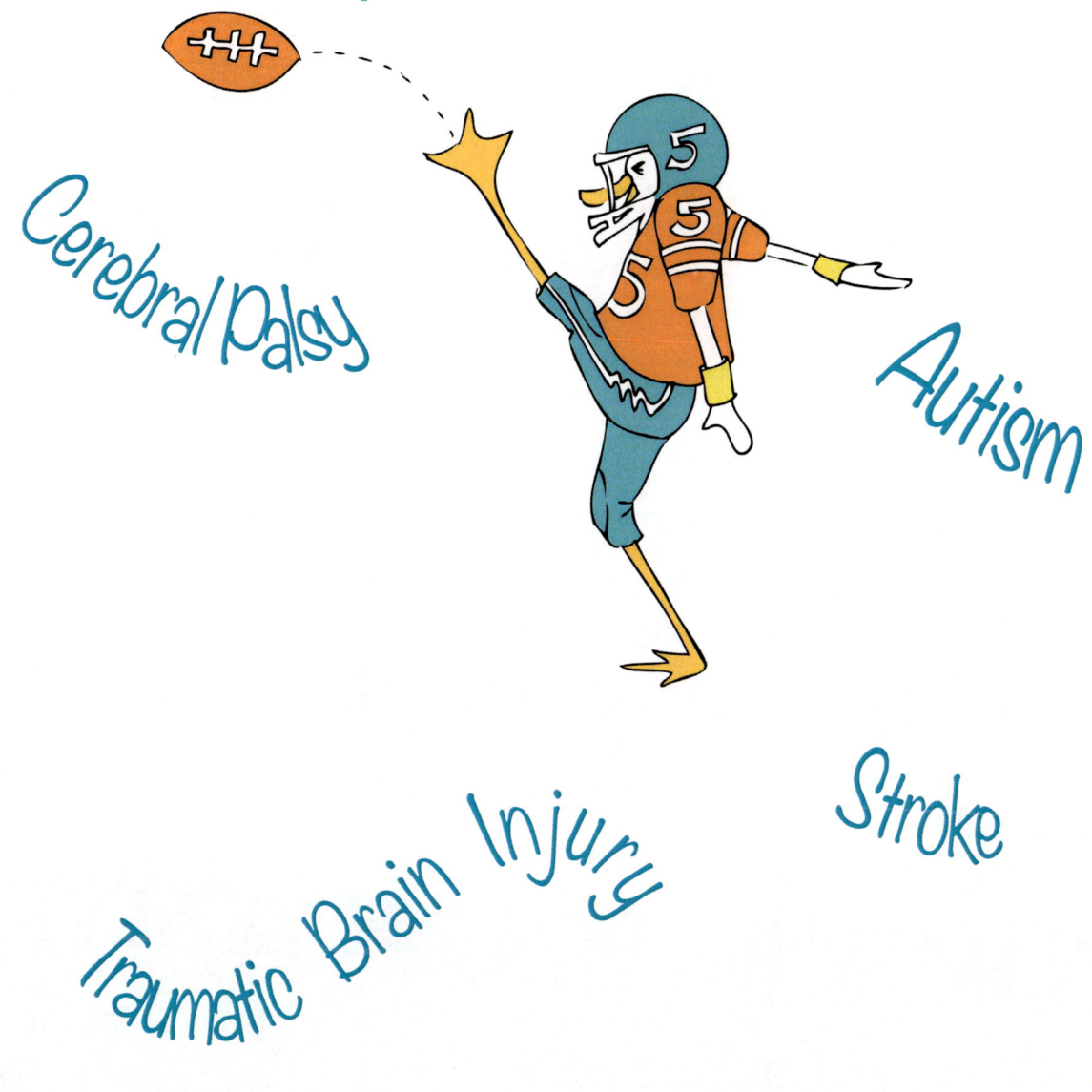

Cerebral Palsy

Autism

Stroke

Traumatic Brain Injury

We all like to socialize and sports offer us a chance to be a part of a team. If playing sports is not for you, how about trying a fantasy sport? There are so many opportunities for communication and fun!

Graham is a sports guy. He loves any sport he can watch. If he could he would probably talk about sports facts all the time. I wanted to find a way for Graham to participate in conversations with his dad and brothers especially around the topic of "Fantasy Football" so he didn't feel left out. So we programmed his device. Now he gets to talk sports, and feel part of a team.

He picked players for his Fantasy Football team using his device. He watches the real football games on TV to see how his players are doing. So in addition to talking about weekly stats, there is more time with family watching the live games, more talk about whose player did well and how many points were scored and tons more communication.

What if your loved one does not have a device? CHAT Collective has designed a communication system to help you socialize with your child, parent or grandparent that has a communication challenge. You can help them engage in sports talk or join a fantasy football team too.

Having more than one way to communicate is really important.

What if it rains . . .
does your device work in the rain?
What if your batteries run out . . .
do you have a back up plan?
Can you use your device in the car?
In the pool? In the snow?
How many tools are in your toolbox?

Always be prepared!

CHAT Collective Identification Products

The CHAT Collective ID product line was developed to help identify individuals with communication challenges.

These products were designed to prevent crises like that faced by a real family whose young son, a limited communicator, was accidentally left behind on a field trip to an amusement park and was lost for six hours with no way of contacting his parents or asking for help.

If the LC had a CHAT Collective ID Tag his parents would have been called much sooner!

One day a boy and his dad went skiing. The boy was a limited communicator. He looks like a typical teenager. They were riding up the lift when a scary thing happened. The boy fell off the lift. His dad could not jump off because the lift went higher and it was too dangerous. The boy was alone on the mountain.

While he was physically okay,
he was lost and alone and could not tell anyone.
His words were limited.

A very nice person asked the boy
if he wanted help to get back on the lift.
The boy said okay.

So he got on the lift.
He did not know how to put the bar down to be safe.
He rode the lift up the mountain by himself without the safety bar. He was okay, but his dad was very upset he was put on the lift alone.

If the boy had a CHAT Collective ID tag on his coat, the person that offered to help him would have seen that he was a limited communicator and hopefully called the number on the tag to get the boy help.

It is so easy to be separated from a loved one that has a communication challenge. Identification is super important!

Susie is a nonverbal communicator. She is an adult and she wanted to go to the mall. A lot of times Susie has a personal assistant or family member travel with her. This time Susie wanted to do it by herself. She looked up the bus routes and times and got on a bus. She waited and waited for her stop but she never got to the mall because this bus was the wrong bus.

Susie could not tell anyone with her voice that she was on the wrong bus. The bus driver knew she did not get off and wondered if there was something wrong.

Susie was wearing a CHAT Collective ID tag. The bus driver saw it and called the number to get Susie help. Susie made it to the mall after all!

The ID Tags can be affixed to clothing, zippers, backpacks and/or other equipment and each provides space to list an emergency phone number.

If you have difficulty being understood or cannot speak at all, you can wear a **CHAT Collective ID Tag** or **Dog Tag** to indicate that you are a NVC/LC.

If you know someone who is a NVC/LC, he or she can wear these products to help alert others.

These are especially useful to medical and emergency staff who are trained to look for identification information.

Be a CHAT Collective Ambassador

Graham and I believe that **CHAT Collective Ambassadors** will spread the word that everyone can communicate and help the verbal community learn how to communicate with us!

We need your help to share and spread the message that everyone can communicate! If you know someone who is a nonverbal or limited communicator please tell them about our message. They can go to this website: **www.chatcollective.com** to learn more about communication.

You can be a part of our **CHAT Collective Team** too! Tell your teacher or family about CHAT Collective. Help your classmates, friends and family members to communicate by teaching them how by using our communication devices.

Help spread our message

The End

Call to Action:

In the spirit that everyone communicates, help us ...

- Consider purchasing another copy of this book for your organization, family member or library.

- Buy a bulk book order at a discount and do a fundraiser for your church, agency or group.

- You aren't alone. Share your experience at our community page at www.chatcollective.com

- Therapists & Educators – we know your passion to make a difference. Thank you. More resources can be found at www.chatcollective.com as Tools for Therapists and Teachers.

www.chatcollective.com

Give the Gift of Communication

Acknowledgements

I would like to thank all of you who contributed to this book through our connections and experiences on this crazy roller coaster ride we call life.

To my guys: Greg, Colby, Tysen and Graham: I love you with all my heart! To Beth Tollar: Thank you for opening your heart to our family and sharing your family with us. Your ability to work with people with communication challenges changed our lives. You think everyone sees the world like you do, treating all people equally and I hope this book will help them to do just that. Thanks for staying on this crazy ride with us through a lot of tough times. To Dr John Upledger thank you for loving Graham, loving me, and for developing craniosacral therapy which has impacted hundreds of thousands of lives making them one touch better. CST changed our lives and so did you! You told me I would help a lot of people like Graham one day and I hope this book does just that. To Peter Blanck Chairman of the Burton Blatt Institute at Syracuse University: Thank you for believing! From the first time we met you believed in me, and encouraged me to share my stories with the world. To Kate Battoe: I treasure our friendship and feel a special connection to you that leaves me smiling and happy every time we are together. To Marilyn and Brett: Thank you for being special friends and touching my life. To Lydia: Thank you for years of creativity and fun developing so many wonderful projects together. The illustrations, design layout and photos gave the guidebook the whimsical touch that we both love!

To my brother Bill: thanks for being you! You are such a big part of Graham's enjoyment in the fantasy football league.....you have a special relationship through email that is so wonderful to see. He loves trash talking with you ! To The 2012 CHAT Camp and the 2013 CHAT Club families and staff: thank you for sharing your time with us and teaching me that what is important to all of us is our connections to each other and knowing you are not alone. To Emily and Brian: thank you for being such great friends to Graham! To Mark and Sherry Russell: for years of friendship, support and fun. Thanks for your creativity through Ayni-Brigade. To Sharon McAuliffe: thanks for supporting me on this wild ride. At our first lunch neither one of us had any idea where this would lead. To Carolyn Phillips: for being there for me since high school and bringing your talents and love to help me achieve this dream. To Katy and Adam: thank you for a dream vacation in Aspen and a beautiful setting to finish this book. To Mary and Andy Tresness: for supporting me through the loss of my parents and all the love and support you have showed me through the years. To my husband Greg: for a wonderful life together. When we met at college when we were 18 years old I could never have imagined the years of happiness we would have together raising a family and seeing our boys grow to be successful young men.

With gratitude and love;

Barb

Based on the belief that "everyone can communicate," CHAT Collective's mission is to inspire and empower society to engage effectively with nonverbal and limited communicators. CHAT Collective, which stands for "Connecting Humans through Awareness and Technique," has developed innovative, low-cost tools and techniques to benefit those who have communications challenges brought on by birth, strokes and traumatic brain or other injuries.

The CHAT Collective Communication System was initially developed to help identify nonverbal and limited communicators, facilitate conversation with them, and create socialization opportunities for them. The suite of convenient and highly effective tools are designed – and have been product-tested by communication specialists.

Founded by disabled rights advocate and the mother of a nonverbal communicator, Barb Tresness, CHAT Collective strives to improve the ability and confidence of families, teachers, healthcare providers and others to interact with and improve the lives of nonverbal and limited communicators.

Connect with Barb and CHAT Collective at www.chatcollective.com

Made in the USA
Middletown, DE
31 October 2015